Aliens at the Fun Fair

Ziggy and Pod had dressed up as
humans.

"Our mission today is to find out
what humans do for fun," said Ziggy.

"OK, boss," said Pod.

The aliens saw a poster.

FUN FAIR! FUN FOR ALL THE FAMILY!

"We will go to the fun fair!" said Ziggy.
"Then we will find out what humans
do for fun."

"Is my human costume OK?" asked Pod. "I have got two arms, two legs and two heads."

"You fool!" said Ziggy. "Humans only have *one* head!"
"Sorry, boss," said Pod.

The aliens saw some young humans holding balloons.

"Why are they holding those round things on string?" asked Pod.

"I think it is to stop the round things from getting away," said Ziggy.

"Good thinking, boss," said Pod.

A boy was crying.

"I want a balloon," he cried.

Ziggy wanted to help. He gave the boy lots of balloons. The boy floated up into the air.

"That doesn't look like fun," said Pod.

The aliens went over to the coconut shy.

"What are those little creatures doing?" asked Pod.

"Let's watch and see," said Ziggy.

"Good thinking, boss," said Pod.

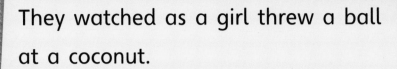

They watched as a girl threw a ball at a coconut.

"Did you see that?" asked Ziggy.

"She hit that poor little creature on the head."

"That doesn't look like fun," said Pod.

The aliens went over to the dodgems. "Look, they are crashing those cars," said Ziggy. "Are they supposed to do that?"

"Well, it doesn't look like fun to me," said Pod.

Next, the aliens bought some candy floss.
"This tastes very odd," said Ziggy.
"Why do humans eat it? It tastes like cotton wool!"

Next, Ziggy and Pod went on the giant roller-coaster.

First, the roller-coaster went up, up, up.

Then it went down – **very**, **very** fast.

Ziggy and Pod screamed and screamed.

Do you think roller-coasters are fun?

"That was no fun at all," said Pod.
"No," said Ziggy, "but it does show
what candy floss is for. It is for humans
to throw out of their mouths after going
on the roller-coaster!"

"Fun fairs are not fun," said Ziggy.
"I never want to eat candy floss again," said Pod.

The aliens went back to their spaceship to write their mission report.
They were glad to leave the fun fair.

MISSION REPORT TO HOME PLANET

Visit to Fun Fair

Humans throw things at little creatures.

They crash cars.

They scream and scream on the
roller-coaster and then they throw
the candy floss out of their mouths.

And they call that fun!

Quiz

Text Detective

- Why didn't the aliens think the dodgems were fun?
- What rides do you like at a fun fair?

Word Detective

- Phonic Focus: Adding 'ing' to verbs ending in 'e'
  Page 15: Which letter must be dropped from 'leave' before adding 'ing'?
- Page 9: Find a word meaning 'looked'.
- Page 11: What words does Ziggy say?

Super Speller

Read these words:

those   doesn't   leaving

Now try to spell them!

HA! HA! HA!

Q How do aliens drink tea?

A Out of flying saucers!

Before Reading

Find out about

- The crazy things people do for fun

Tricky words

- dangerous
- scary
- elastic
- stretches
- special
- soapy
- crawl
- roller-coaster

Introduce these tricky words and help the reader when they come across them later!

Text starter

Bungee Jumping, Scad Diving, Zorbing and Potholing are all crazy sports that some people do for fun! They are dangerous and scary – but that's why people do them!

You Want to do WHAT?

Sometimes people do things for fun
which are dangerous or scary.
Are they brave?
Are they mad?

Bungee Jumping!

Does this sound like fun?

You stand on a very high bridge.

Then you jump off!

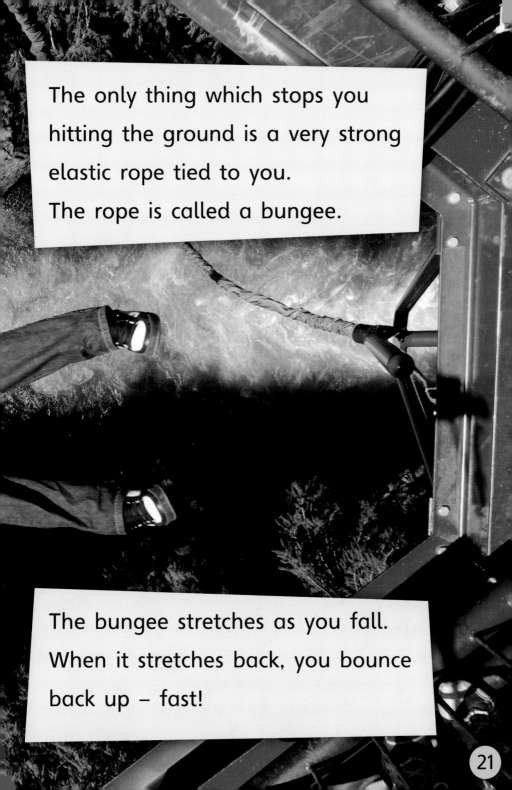

The only thing which stops you hitting the ground is a very strong elastic rope tied to you.
The rope is called a bungee.

The bungee stretches as you fall.
When it stretches back, you bounce back up – fast!

Scad Diving!

Does this sound like fun?

You stand on a very high bridge

or in a helicopter.

Then you jump!

This time, you have no bungee rope,

so you fall and fall ...

Then you drop into a wide net.

Scad Diving is **very** dangerous.

You fall very fast – as fast as a speeding car!

Zorbing!

Does this sound like fun?

You get inside a giant ball.

You are strapped into a special chair and the ball is filled with air.

Then it rolls down a very big hill with you inside it!

Sometimes, there is no special chair.
You are in a small ball inside
the giant ball. Soapy water is put
inside the ball.
As the ball rolls, you fall around
like clothes in a washing machine!
This is called Wet Zorbing.

Potholing!

Does this sound like fun?

You explore caves deep underground.

You crawl from one cave to the next along thin tunnels.

It is very dark so you wear a helmet with a light on it. You get very cold and wet.

The biggest danger in underground potholes is flash floods!

Potholing is very dangerous.

You can get lost in very deep caves.

You can get trapped in thin tunnels.

You can drown in a cave which
has filled with water.

Banger Racing

Does this sound like fun?

You are strapped into a car. Then you race around the track as fast as you can. You must watch out for other cars which might smash into you!

Banger Racing is very dangerous.
Your car gets smashed up, but you
might get smashed up too!

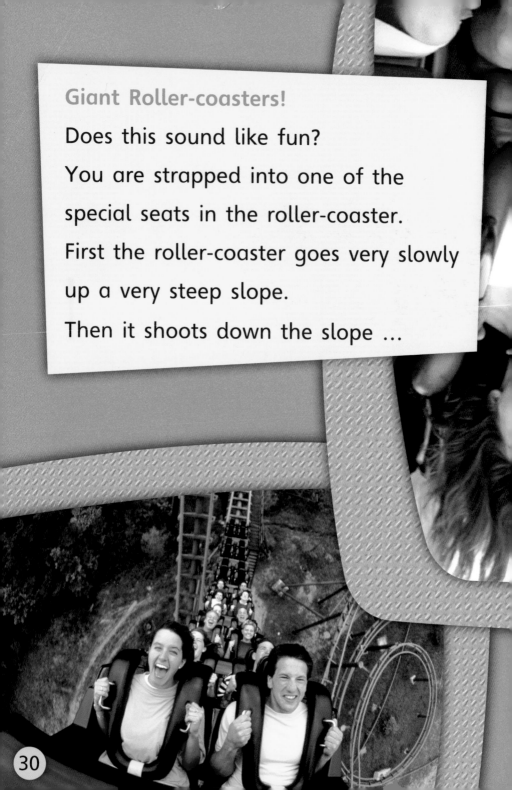

Giant Roller-coasters!

Does this sound like fun?

You are strapped into one of the special seats in the roller-coaster.

First the roller-coaster goes very slowly up a very steep slope.

Then it shoots down the slope ...

The roller-coaster twists and turns.
Sometimes it goes upside down!
Sometimes it goes backwards!

Some people say these things are fun.
Are they brave or mad?
What do you say?

Quiz

Text Detective

- Why is potholing sometimes dangerous?
- Which activity do you think is the scariest?

Word Detective

- **Phonic Focus:** Adding 'ing' to verbs ending in 'e'
  Page 28: Which letter must be dropped from 'race'
  before adding 'ing'?
- Page 22: Why does the last line end in ... ?
- Page 30: Find two smaller words in 'roller-coaster'.

Super Speller

Read these words:

trapped   **racing**   **might**

Now try to spell them!

HA! HA! HA!

Q What happened to the man who jumped off a bridge in Paris?

A He went in Seine!